T0022752

The CTURNALS

PRESENTS

Nighttime Animals

Awesome Features & Surprising Adaptations

by
Tracey Hecht

Fabled Films Press
New York

Published by Fabled Films LLC, New York

ISBN: 978-1-944020-71-2

Library of Congress Control Number: 2021950123

First Edition: October 2022

1 3 5 7 9 10 8 6 4 2

Book produced by WonderLab Group, LLC
Science writing by Laura Marsh
Designed by Project Design Company
Photo edited by Annette Kiesow
Character illustrations by Josie Yee

Educational reviews by Dr. Erica Colón, Catherine Jacobs, and Lauren Woodrow

Typeset in Mrs. Ant, Stemple Garamond, and Benton Sans
Printed by Everbest in China

FABLED FILMS PRESS
NEW YORK CITY
fabledfilms.com

For information on bulk purchases for promotional use please contact Fabled Films Press Sales department at info@fabledfilms.com.

Note to Reader

Throughout the book, you will see important **vocabulary words in bold type**. You can find the meaning of these words in the Word Glossary on page 57.

TABLE OF CONTENTS

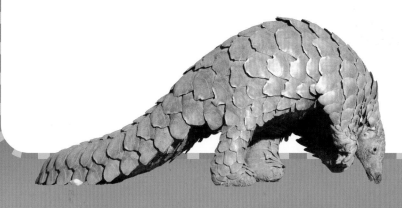

Meet
The Nocturnals

It was dark and much of the world was asleep.
But a special group of animals were wide
awake…The Nocturnals!

Bismark the sugar glider landed near the group's usual meeting spot. Tobin the pangolin walked over on his two hind legs. Then Dawn the red fox appeared with a flick of her long, bushy tail.

"Welcome, my fine friends!" said Bismark.

Tobin stretched as if he had just woken up. "I'm excited to explore the nighttime world this evening! Maybe we'll even make some new friends."

"Animals that come out in the dark are really special," said Dawn. "They have unique skills and fabulous features!"

"Well, what are we waiting for? Let's get going!" Bismark yelled excitedly as he led the way into the dark night.

Introducing the Nighttime World

While most of the world goes to sleep, **nocturnal** animals are just getting started. A whole other world comes alive after dark!

Nocturnal animals have important **adaptations** for living life in the darkness. Some have terrific sight or hearing. Others have a keen sense of touch or sense of smell. These adaptations allow them to stay safe from predators and find food—all in the dark. Nocturnal animals live in different areas of the world. Even if they live on opposite sides of the planet, these animals are connected by their nighttime lives.

SUGAR GLIDER

WHY NOT PLAY DURING THE DAY?

Sleeping during the day and being active at night is usually safer for animals. Fewer large **predators** are active at night. Also, fewer animals are searching for food at night. So there is more to go around. In hot areas like the desert, many nocturnal animals snooze during the warmest part of the day. This means they lose less water from their bodies, which helps them to survive.

RED FOX

PANGOLIN

7

"Ladies and gentlemen," Bismark announced. "I present: myself! The sugar glider!" Bismark took a deep, low bow. "Lots of nocturnal animals have awesome athletic abilities—like me, for example!"

"I agree," said Tobin. "You can really get around."

"Whoa! Look at that sugar glider soar!" shouted Bismark.

8

CHAPTER 1

Awesome Athletic Abilities

Nocturnal animals have some surprising adaptations. Gliding, jumping, and running are just a few of their awesome abilities.

Meet the Soaring Sugar Glider

A sugar glider doesn't exactly fly like a superhero. But it can glide gracefully through the night air.

It takes a springing leap—and then it soars. Thin skin attached to its wrists and ankles acts like a parachute.

In the air, a sugar glider's long, bushy tail helps it to steer. Before landing, all four limbs come forward. Sharp claws grab on to the tree or branch where it lands.

Leaping and gliding from tree to tree help keep the sugar glider safe. That's because many of its predators are on the ground.

Fun Fact

When danger is near, a sugar glider makes a barking sound like a small dog. This sounds the alarm for others: Watch out!

STICKING TOGETHER

During the day, sugar gliders sleep in a cozy nest made of leaves. They build the nest in a hollow of a tree. Up to 10 adults and their young will stay in one nest. When it gets cold, they huddle together to sleep and stay warm.

INCREDIBLE EYES

A sugar glider's large black eyes help
it survive, too. Big eyes let in more
light so it can see well in the darkness.
These eyes can spot predators and
help it see where it's going at night.

At night, sharp eyes also help a sugar glider find food. Sugar gliders get their name from the sweet foods they eat, such as tree sap, pollen, and flower nectar. They also eat insects, spiders, lizards, eggs, and small birds.

Since the sugar glider sleeps in the trees and finds its food there, too, there aren't many reasons to come down to the ground.

I can catch a flying insect in midair! How's that for an awesome athletic ability?

Meet the Clever Kinkajou

At night, if a kinkajou runs
into a predator, it has a
great getaway move. It can
change the direction of its feet—
without moving its upper body! The kinkajou
runs the other way in a flash.

Large predators can climb the trees the kinkajou lives in. So the kinkajou's fancy footwork helps it avoid becoming dinner!

Fun Fact

It may look like a monkey. But a kinkajou is more closely related to a raccoon.

Being able to rotate its feet and run isn't the kinkajou's only athletic ability. It can also hang upside down by its tail like a monkey.

Almost like another hand, the kinkajou's tail grabs things. This kind of tail is called **prehensile**. A kinkajou can grasp a tree limb with its tail while eating fruit with one hand. Its tail also helps the kinkajou balance.

SWEET TOOTH

Kinkajous mostly eat fruit. They also eat insects, flowers, and nectar. They even raid beehives looking for honey. That's how the kinkajou got its nickname, "honey bear." Luckily, the kinkajou's short, thick fur protects it from bee stings.

Terrific Tails

A kinkajou is just one nighttime animal with a terrific tail. Check out these other fantastic nocturnal animal tails!

POSSUM

Unlike some other possum species, the common brushtail possum has a long, bushy tail. It can be longer than half the length of the possum's body. On the underside of the tail there is a spot with no hair. This helps the possum grab onto tree branches.

SUGAR GLIDER

Who needs a bucket when you have a tail? When building a nest, the sugar glider uses its tail to carry leaves. The tail also keeps the animal balanced as it runs quickly along tree branches.

PANGOLIN

Ever heard of a pangolin taxi? Baby black-bellied pangolins catch a ride on their mother's tail. The adults also use their tails to grip branches while climbing trees. And when they move quickly on their two hind feet, their tails keep them balanced, too.

Meet the Fabulous Fox

In a bright red flash, a fox jumps straight up in the air—as high as six feet (1.8 m)! Its body makes an upside-down U shape in the air. Then the fox brings its front paws straight down. This pins down its meal, so it won't get away.

FLEXIBLE FOXES

Foxes are mostly active at night. But they can be active at dawn and dusk, too. If foxes are in a safe place, sometimes they even come out during the day.

Foxes eat just about everything, including rodents, rabbits, insects, and lizards. They also eat fruit, fish, and grasses. Eating so many different foods helps foxes live in many **habitats**. Foxes live throughout the world.

"Not only can Dawn jump like a champion," explained Bismark, "but she has super hearing, too. She can hear me coming almost a mile away! Can you believe it?"

Dawn chuckled. "Yes, I do have strong hearing, Bismark. Now hear this!"

CHAPTER 2

Sensational Senses

Nocturnal animals have adapted to hear, see, smell, and feel their way through the dark. Their sensational **senses** help them find food, too.

A red fox has fantastic hearing. Its pointed ears stick up and easily catch sound. The ears also move separately from each other. They allow the fox to hear from the side as well as from behind.

Fun Fact

Red foxes are not always red. They can be rusty orange, pale yellow, gray, or black.

23

A red fox can see well in low light. But it relies more on its great hearing to hunt. It can hear a small mouse moving under snow or leaves more than 40 feet (12 m) away. That's farther than the length of a school bus!

The red fox's powerful ears can target exactly where its prey is. Then it pounces.

BAT-EARED FOX

FENNEC FOX

WHAT BIG EARS YOU HAVE!

Other mostly nocturnal fox species, such as bat-eared foxes, fennec foxes, and kit foxes, have big ears, too. In Africa, ears on the bat-eared fox and fennec fox are large for their bodies. The bat-eared fox can hear the soft sound of scurrying termites. The fennec fox can hear insects moving quietly under the desert sand. And in North America, the ears on a kit fox allow it to find kangaroo rat burrows underground.

KIT FOX

Red foxes have a great sense of smell, too. This helps them find prey in the dark. But they also use their sense of smell another way.

When foxes have more food than they can scarf down, they hide it for later. This is called caching. Foxes cache their food by burying it under dirt, leaves, or snow. They may also stash it in a den. It's like having their own refrigerator! When they're hungry again, they use their super sniffers to find the food. Then they dig it up.

COZY DENS

Foxes usually use dens only in wet weather or when raising babies. Most dens are underground. They can also be between big rocks or in hollow logs.

Fun Fact

A fox often stalks its prey like a cat. It can run up to 30 miles an hour (48 km/h) to catch a meal.

Meet the Bold Bat

Throughout the world, there are more than 1,400 different species of bats. Most bat species are microbats.

GREY LONG-EARED BAT

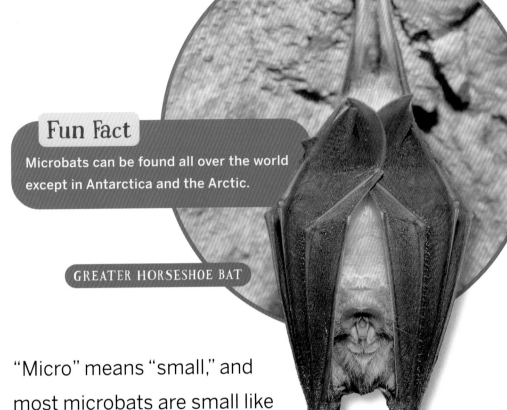

GREATER HORSESHOE BAT

"Micro" means "small," and most microbats are small like their name. Many microbats have tiny eyes that don't see well at night. Instead these bats have excellent hearing, and many have big ears to catch sound.

A microbat's great sense of hearing helps it get around in the dark. It also helps the bat find food to eat. This is a good thing because most microbats eat their body weight—or more—in insects every night.

Microbats have a superpower sense called **echolocation**.

Here's how it works: Microbats make a series of sounds through their noses or mouths. Then they listen for the sound to bounce off an object and echo back to them. From this echo, the bats can tell how far away the object is.

Echolocation helps microbats find insects to eat. It also helps them avoid anything in their way, like trees.

Fun Fact

Many microbats have a flap of skin called a nose leaf. Scientists think the nose leaf may help microbats focus their sound during echolocation.

Marvelous Megabats

"Mega" means "big," and these types of bats can be huge! Get ready to meet the largest megabat of them all, the flying fox.

GRAY-HEADED FLYING FOX

FABULOUS FLYING FOXES

Flying foxes are a kind of megabat. They are bats with faces that look like foxes. They have pointed ears, large black noses, long snouts, and fuzzy fur. The largest flying foxes have **wingspans** that are more than five feet (1.5 m) wide, and they can weigh up to 3.5 pounds (1.5 kg)!

INDIAN FLYING FOX

HANGING AROUND

Flying foxes hang upside down when they **roost**. Their long sharp claws are curved, so they can easily hang on.

FINDING FOOD

Unlike microbats, megabats don't use echolocation to get around. Their big eyes see very well in the dark. At night, they use their sight and great sense of smell to find food. Megabats mostly eat nectar, pollen, and fruit. That's why they are also called fruit bats.

LYLE'S FLYING FOXES

Fun Fact

A group of roosting flying foxes is called a camp.

Meet the Sneaky Snake

A snake doesn't use its nostrils to smell. Instead, it smells with its tongue. A snake flicks its tongue in and out of its mouth. It is picking up **scents** in the air. This helps the snake find food and avoid predators.

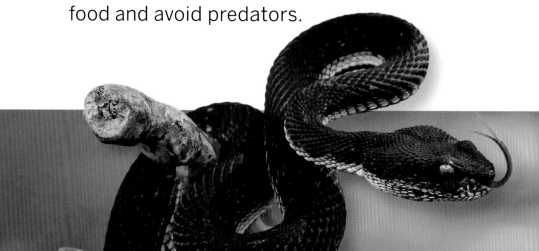

Snakes have other ways to sense their surroundings, too. Snakes called pit vipers have small holes, or pits, near their mouths and eyes. These are sensors that feel heat. In the dark, a pit viper can feel the heat of another animal. The snake can tell where its predator or prey is without seeing it.

A DIFFERENT WAY OF "HEARING"

Snakes don't have ears on the outside of their heads like we do. Instead, they "hear" by feeling sound. When a rodent rustles nearby, the sound travels through the ground. Snakes can feel this through bones in their lower jaws. Then they know that dinner is nearby.

"Oh, my! That's special what a snake can do," said Bismark.

"But there's more," Dawn said. "Our nocturnal bodies can be helpful in many interesting ways."

"Good thing I'm so brave and can handle this snake's special features," said Bismark in a wobbly voice. "And you thought I had a big mouth…Wait till you see this!"

CHAPTER 3

Bizarre Bodies

The bodies of nocturnal animals adapt to their habitats to give them an advantage at night.

Snakes won't win any prizes for good table manners. Because they can't chew, they swallow their food whole. Their flexible jaws allow them to swallow prey that is much bigger than the size of their heads. And this big "bite" takes a while to go down.

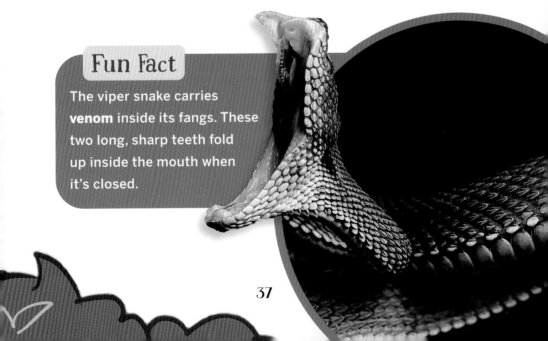

Fun Fact

The viper snake carries **venom** inside its fangs. These two long, sharp teeth fold up inside the mouth when it's closed.

Meet the Playful Possum

Do you see the reddish stain on the common brushtail possum's chest? The possum didn't spill ketchup on itself. That stain is made by its scent gland. To mark its territory, the male possum rubs its scent on trees in its home area. Then other possums know they're not welcome to move in.

SAY WHAT?

Common brushtail possums have a lot to say at night! Since they're nocturnal, this is when they "talk" to each other. They hiss, screech, grunt, chatter, cough, and click. They are sending warnings, looking for a mate, and telling others where their territory is.

Marsupial Moms

Human parents may sometimes carry their babies in slings or backpacks. But marsupials are mammals with a built-in baby carrier! These animal moms have special pouches on the outside of their bodies, perfect for bringing their babies everywhere, even in the dark.

Fun Fact

About 330 **species** of marsupials live in Australia and South America today. Only one species lives in North America: the opossum.

ROCK WALLABIES

RIGHT AFTER BIRTH, the tiny baby called a joey crawls into its mother's pouch. A newborn joey is deaf and blind and has very little hair. In the pouch, the baby stays safe and warm. It drinks its mother's milk while it grows and develops.

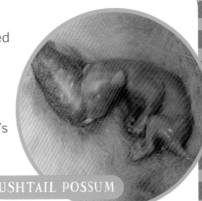

BRUSHTAIL POSSUM

WOMBATS

AFTER SEVERAL MONTHS, the much bigger joey is ready to leave the pouch. It won't leave its mother yet. First it needs to learn how to find food and avoid predators.

WHEN A JOEY GROWS TOO LARGE for the pouch, the young marsupial sometimes sticks on mom. Some babies will cling to their mom's back instead of weighing down the pouch.

SUGAR GLIDERS

Speaking of marsupials, wombats have a wild and wacky pouch!

It's true. We do.

Meet the Wonderful Wombat

Like other marsupials, female wombats have a pouch to carry their babies. But the wombat's pouch is unusual. Instead of facing the mother's head, it faces backward—toward her behind.

And that's lucky for her joey! Wombats dig with their front paws. They throw a lot of loose dirt and sand behind them like a snow blower. By facing backward, the joey doesn't get hit in the face by flying debris.

Fun Fact

The bare-nosed wombat is the only animal on Earth that makes cube-shaped poop!

"Our powerful nocturnal bodies help us rule the night," said Bismark. "We are bold! We are brave! We are fierce!"

"Even those of us who are not fierce have many great ways to protect ourselves," said Dawn.

"Oh, yes! Like Chandler's great escape moves," said Tobin. "You do not want to miss this fur-ocious defense!"

CHAPTER 4

Powerful Protections

Nocturnal animals have special defenses to help them get away from predators safely.

Meet the Cozy Chinchilla

A chinchilla has thick fur that keeps it warm in the mountains where it lives. If a predator bites a chinchilla, it can release the patch of fur that's being bitten. Then the chinchilla can run away, while the predator is left with a mouthful of fur. This tricky move is called a fur slip.

Meet the Proud Pangolin

A pangolin looks like it's ready for battle. Armor-like scales cover its body from the top of its head to the tip of its tail. These hard scales are made of keratin, the same stuff that our fingernails are made of.

When threatened, a pangolin rolls into a tight ball. The hard scales are on the outside. Its soft, hairy belly is protected on the inside. Most predators decide not to bother with it and walk away—even lions! During the day, some nocturnal pangolins sleep curled in a ball with their babies tucked inside.

Fun Fact

Baby pangolins are born with soft scales, which harden about three days after birth.

Hopefully, you don't get a whiff of my other form of protection...

A pangolin has a strong sense of smell for finding insects in the dark. It also creates a strong smell as a defense! When danger is near, a pangolin releases a smelly fluid from a gland near its tail. The smell is so awful that most predators don't want to stick around.

PROTECTING PANGOLINS

Pangolins are the most **trafficked** animals in the world. In some countries, they are used to make traditional medicines. Although it's against the law, pangolins are killed and sold in large numbers. The more people learn about pangolins, the more we can do to protect them.

Fun Fact

In some pangolin species, the tongue is as long as the body. Inside the pangolin, the tongue runs all the way through the chest. It attaches near the bottom ribs.

A pangolin's super long tongue allows it to eat its favorite nighttime meal: ants and termites. These insects live in long, thin tunnels and holes. Since a pangolin's tongue is super sticky, termites and ants cling to it like glue.

Pangolins don't have teeth. Instead, small stones in their stomach break down the food they eat.

CLOSED TO ATTACKERS

Ants will attack an animal that invades their **colony**. Luckily, the pangolin has special features to protect it. Thick eyelids cover its eyes. Strong muscles seal off the nose and ears. And almost nothing can get through its thick scales. A pangolin can eat about 70 million insects a year.

Hide-and-Sleep

Predators that are active during the day are searching for their next meal. Since this is when nocturnal animals usually sleep, they need to be hidden from predators. Check out some of the best daytime hiding spots for nighttime animals.

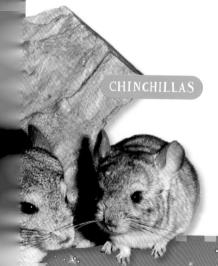

CHINCHILLAS

BETWEEN ROCKS

Chinchillas will den in holes among rocks, as well as in burrows. They usually live in family groups or colonies, sometimes with over 100 chinchillas.

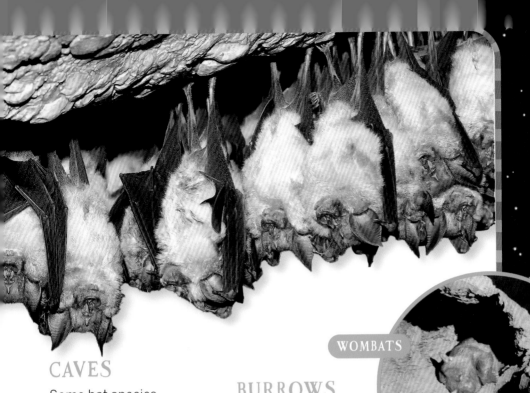

CAVES

Some bat species also sleep in caves. They may roost with thousands—and even millions—of other bats.

BURROWS

Wombats, chinchillas, and pangolins sleep in burrows. Pangolins line their cozy burrows with plants.

WOMBATS

TREES

Sugar gliders and some species of pangolins sleep in tree hollows during the day. Some bat species sleep in trees as well. Hidden from predators, sugar gliders' nests are made of leaves in the trees.

SUGAR GLIDER

The Nocturnals
Until Next Time...

The animals talked excitedly about all they had seen in the nighttime world.

"Dawn, could you teach me how to jump straight up in the air?" asked Bismark.

"Well, Bismark, could you teach me how to glide from tree to tree?" asked Tobin.

Dawn smiled at them and said, "You—and all of the nocturnal animals—should feel proud just the way you are."

The Nocturnals looked at each other and smiled. Dawn was right. They were each special in their own way.

"Three cheers for The Nocturnals!" Bismark called out to the sky.

Nighttime Animal Resources

Want to learn more about nocturnal animals? With the help of a grown-up, explore these books, sites, and videos.

Learn More About Nocturnal Animals

Find animal profiles for bats, kinkajous, pangolins, sugar gliders, and wombats here: animals.sandiegozoo.org/animals

Find out more about Australia and the incredible animals that live there from these museums: australian.museum/learn/animals & qm.qld.gov.au

Learn more about endangered nocturnal animals on the IUCN Red List of Threatened Species: iucnredlist.org

Learn more about pangolins and how you can help the most trafficked mammal in the world: savepangolins.org & worldwildlife.org/species/pangolin

Watch Awesome Nocturnal Animal Videos

Watch a pangolin dig in the dirt: youtu.be/7GQF7iFQQok

See new fox kits and explore how they grow up: youtu.be/uIR_vSRASxM

Listen to the noises a sugar glider makes: youtu.be/8ghzy4w-WKk

See a bat drink from a flower: pbs.org/wnet/nature/blog/bat-fact-sheet

Read About Surprising Nocturnal Adaptations

"Nighttime Animal Behavior: The Moon Has Power Over Animals"
sciencenewsforstudents.org/article/moon-has-power-over-animals

"Scientists Seek Bat Detectives"
sciencenewsforstudents.org/blog/eureka-lab/scientists-seek-bat-detectives

Word Glossary

adaptation: a change that makes a plant or animal better able to live in its environment

colony: animals of one kind that live closely together

echolocation: the process of locating objects by using sound waves that bounce off the object and come back

habitat: the home or area where a plant or animal naturally lives

nocturnal: mostly active at night

predator: an animal that hunts and eats other animals

prehensile: able to grasp and support weight

roost: to settle down with others to rest or sleep, especially for bats or birds

scent: a specific smell

sense: the ability of sight, hearing, smell, taste, or touch

species: a type or category of animal

trafficked: bought or sold illegally

venom: a kind of poison that enters the body through an animal's bite or sting

wingspan: the measurement from tip to tip of bird wings or bat wings

Animal Glossary

Bat

Greater horseshoe bats get their name from
the horseshoe shape of their nose leaf. These
microbats are found in India, Turkey, Israel, and
Jordan, as well as in parts of Africa, Europe, and
Asia. They live in forests, grasslands, shrubland, and
caves. At roosting sites, these bats hang upside down in groups.
Losing their habitat and chemicals used on crops are the biggest
dangers to them. Their numbers are currently okay in the wild.

Read more about bats in *The Best Burp*.

Chinchilla

Long-tailed chinchillas are rodents that live
in the high Andes of South America. They
are mostly nocturnal. They live in groups
and make dens in between rocks. Because
of their thick, soft fur, they have been hunted by
poachers and caught to sell as pets. They are endangered.

Read more about chinchillas in *The Chestnut Challenge*.

Kinkajou

Kinkajous live in trees in the tropical forests of Central and South America. They live in small groups. With their prehensile tails, they can hang from tree limbs. Their reversible feet  let them climb in either direction, and down a tree headfirst! Scent glands near their jaws, throats, and bellies are used to mark their territory. Kinkajous are not endangered animals.

Read more about kinkajous in *The Kooky Kinkajou*.

Pangolin

Pangolins are found in Africa and Southeast Asia. All eight species of pangolin are covered in hard scales. They have long snouts and tongues, which help them eat ants and termites. Most pangolins stick close to the 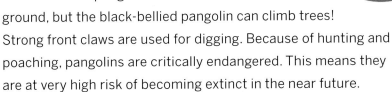 ground, but the black-bellied pangolin can climb trees! Strong front claws are used for digging. Because of hunting and poaching, pangolins are critically endangered. This means they are at very high risk of becoming extinct in the near future.

Read more about pangolins in *The Nocturnals Grow & Read* book series.

Possum

Common brushtail possums are marsupials found throughout Australia and New Zealand. They mostly live in the trees in forests and woodlands. They usually live alone, but may share sleeping places. Scent glands near their chests, chins, and tails are used to mark their territory. Possums are not endangered animals.

Read more about possums in *The Peculiar Possum.*

Red Fox

Red foxes are found all over the world. They can live in deserts, mountains, and even cities. While many red foxes have reddish brown fur, their coat color can also be pale yellow, gray, or black. Red foxes are mostly nocturnal, but can be active at dusk and dawn, and even sometimes during the day. Red foxes are losing habitats, though they are doing well in the wild.

Read more about red foxes in *The Nocturnals Grow & Read* book series.

Snake

Mangrove pit vipers are found in India, Bangladesh, and Southeast Asia. They live in forests and wetlands. They have long fangs and powerful venom. Pits near their eyes sense heat from other animals. Losing their habitat and pollution are dangers to these vipers. Yet they are doing well in the wild.

Read more about snakes in *The Slithery Shakedown.*

Sugar Glider

Sugar gliders are rodents found in Australia,
New Zealand, and Papua New Guinea. They are
known for soaring more than 150 feet (45 m)
from tree to tree. Sugar gliders do this by using a
special kind of skin like a parachute. It is attached at the
sugar glider's front feet and back ankles. Sugar gliders nest in groups.
Males mark group members with scent glands. They use sounds to
"talk" to each other. Sugar gliders are not endangered animals.

Read more about sugar gliders in *The Nocturnals Grow & Read* book series.

Wombat

Wombats are marsupials only found in a few
small areas of Australia. Their stocky bodies
help them dig burrows with long tunnels.
Sometimes they sunbathe during the day outside
their tunnels, but they are mostly nocturnal.
Loss of their woodland and grassland habitat is
the biggest danger to the three wombat species. The northern
hairy-nosed wombat will likely go extinct in the wild in the near
future. The southern hairy-nosed wombat is doing better, but is
still in danger. The common wombat is doing well in the wild.

Read more about wombats in *The Weeping Wombat.*

About the Author

Tracey Hecht is a writer and entrepreneur who has written, directed and produced for film. She created a Nocturnals Read Aloud Writing Program in partnership with the New York Public Library that has expanded nationwide. Tracey splits her time between Oquossoc, Maine, and New York City, with her husband and four children.

About the Science Writer

Laura Marsh has written more than 30 nonfiction books for children. Her work is featured in Lucy Calkins' Units of Study for Teaching Reading, workshop curriculum developed with Teachers College Reading and Writing Project. She lives in Westchester County, New York, with her husband, two sons, and their dog, Bode.

About Fabled Films & Fabled Films Press

Fabled Films is a publishing and entertainment company that creates original content for young readers and middle-grade audiences. Fabled Films Press combines strong literary properties with high quality production values to connect books with generations of parents and their children. The book program was developed under the supervision of science educators and reading specialists to develop kids' reading skills and support national science standards. Each property is supported by websites, educator guides and activities for bookstores, educators, and librarians, as well as videos, social media content, and supplemental entertainment for additional platforms.

FABLED FILMS PRESS
NEW YORK CITY
Connect with Fabled Films and The Nocturnals:
www.NocturnalsWorld.com | www.fabledfilms.com
Facebook | Instagram: @NocturnalsWorld
Twitter: @fabled_films

Photo Credits